CHAMONIX CRAGGING

Valley rock climbs around the area

Nigel Shepherd

CORDEE

ISBN 1 871890 22 5

British Library Cataloguing in Publication Data
A catalogue record for this book is available from the British Library

All trade enquiries to:
Cordee, 3a De Montfort Street, Leicester LE1 7HD

This book is available from all specialist equipment shops and major booksellers. It can, along with all the maps mentioned in the text be obtained direct from the publishers. Please write for a copy of our comprehensive stocklist of outdoor recreation and travel books/maps.

Cover photo: Petit Bargy
Frontispiece photo: Foron-L'ascenceur 7a
Rear cover photo: Rocher des Aravis

Printed and bound in Great Britain by
Butler & Tanner Ltd, Frome and London

CORDEE
3a De Montfort Street, Leicester, Great Britain, LE1 7HD

CONTENTS

INTRODUCTION

For many climbers visiting the Chamonix valley there are days when it's good to take a break from the stresses and strains of alpine climbing or to escape from the incessant rain and just go cragging for a few hours.

Within the valley, and just a short drive out of it, there is a great variety of good rock climbing to be found. Rough gneiss, perfect granite and limestone provide worthwhile climbing, quite often in stunning surroundings and sunny when all else is doom and gloom.

This guide opens up opportunities for climbing that have existed for many years but are not at all well known to visiting climbers. The criteria applied to selecting the climbs centres around those that are within an hour or so driving time of Chamonix; that are relatively easy of access and are equipped with bolt runners and anchors, lower off points and where applicable abseil stations. Driving time is pretty subjective of course and those estimated here are based on ambling along in a 16 valve Golf GTI.

The crags, and many others not included, appear in a variety of guidebooks. To buy all the guidebooks to the area would be very expensive and hardly practical for the visitor. I have included information on the guides and topos that are available so that climbers may, if they wish, acquire definitive information for each crag.

The guide is not intended to be exhaustive and by its nature is a personal selection, but it does contain details of many climbs of all standards from the easiest to the very hardest grades. Throughout the book I have used French grades rather than follow the questionable line of converting each to a British grade. A loose table of grading comparisons is included simply to provoke discussion – which it's bound to do!

The description of how to find each crag and the routes thereon is as succinct as it needs to be. Rather than waffle on with flowery description and anecdote I have attempted to make the guide as practical and user friendly as possible. You will have to use your 'crag sense' to fill in the blank bits.

Access to some of the crags is a delicate affair. Similar to the UK, there are friendly landowners and those that are less so. Notes on access and, particularly parking, relevant to each crag are found in the crag introduction. **Please respect any special arrangements in order not to jeopardise the facility.**

Some of the crags are in nature reserves or areas of special interest and you should be particularly careful to heed local bye-laws. Do not leave litter and try to set an example by not going to the toilet on or near the footpaths.

Wherever possible I have tried to use a photo-topo to illustrate the climbs. There have been occasions when this has neither been practical nor desirable. In such instances it is a simple enough matter to locate the start of each climb mentioned and to follow a line of bolts. Sometimes following lines of bolts is not as straightforward as it might be, particularly where climbs are very close together. The climber will have to use his or her judgement to solve such mysteries on the spot.

Climbs are marked on photos with dotted or dashed lines. These give an indication of the line taken. It is not always possible to photograph crags from 'face on'. Consequently things appear shortened or distorted from certain angles. Similarly, stances, lower offs and abseil points are indicated as accurately as can be achieved.

The increasingly popular and indeed sensible use of pictographs has been used to summarise information on each crag. This is purely a quick reference of the details contained in the text. An explanation of each pictograph used in the book follows this introduction.

The maps and diagrams are simplistically drawn to show only relevant details. For more accurate information you should of course refer to the IGN series of maps which are excellent. In many cases the crags described in this guide are marked on the IGN maps and are thus simple to locate.

Finally, a word for all those who believe that to put a bolt next to a perfect nut crack is sacrilige and spout forth monotonously about it – buy the book by all means but don't go cragging on these crags described. You know it won't be good for your blood pressure . . .

Good climbing!

Nigel Shepherd is a professional mountain guide with more than 22 years experience as a guide and instructor. He was, for a time, the Training Officer to the British Association of Mountain Guides and in 1993 became the President of that association. He has climbed and guided throughout the world and now lives near Llanberis in North Wales from where he runs a guiding business. His writing and photographs have been published widely in the climbing press and is the author of several books including the highly acclaimed 'A Manual of Modern Rope Techniques'.

ACKNOWLEDGEMENTS

No work of this kind can possibly be undertaken without a lot of assistance, encouragement and willing climbing partners.

I am grateful to many people and my thanks are recorded here. I am particularly indebted to those mentioned below;

To Michel at Sports Alpins in Chamonix for the first topo to Chapelle St Gras on the back of a till receipt and for looking over the manuscript.

To Jules for a few climbs but mostly for boundless enthusiasm, advice and monumental hangovers.

To Robert, postman in Servoz and climbing partner on some memorable afternoons.

To Jon de Montjoye for his advice and for looking over and correcting the manuscript..

And to Chrissy for going cragging when she wanted to be on the high peaks. (and for taking the photograph on the back cover.)

This book is for them and everyone who goes cragging.

Nigel Shepherd
North Wales 1995

All photos and topo diagrams in this book are by the author. (Except for the one on the back cover.)

GUIDEBOOK DISCLAIMER

The information on climbs described in this guidebook is gathered from a variety of sources and as such the author cannot assure the reader of the accuracy of any of the information in the book, including the topos, photodiagrams, maps and the graded difficulty of the climbs, descriptions of climbs or any other written information.

The inclusion of a cliff and any climbs described in this book does not indicate a right of access or the right to climb.

The difficulty rating of a climb is a subjective matter and always depend on the climbers ability to climb rock, physical fitness and characteristics, confidence and experience. Rock climbing is a sport in which the risk of serious injury or death is ever present. In using this book you must rely on your own experience and judgement and your capability to make sound and reasoned decisions in the face of adversity.

The topos, photodiagrams and route descriptions included in this guidebook cannot be guaranteed accurate. Lines marked on photos and the use of topos merely give an indication of where the climb might go. Individuals must make their own decisions as to choice of line based on previous experience of rock climbing, personal ability and judgment.

Any in-situ equipment such as bolts, pitons, hangers, threads, chains, abseil cord, rings, cables or nuts are subject to variances in placement, metal fatigue and general degradation. Depending on them for your personal safety carries inherent risks associated with the above mentioned and the user must satisfy him or herself of the suitability and safety of any in situ equipment before entrusting ones life to it. The suggestion that in-situ equipment exists on climbs cannot be substantiated as fact as it may have been removed permanently. To this end you are advised to seek consultation with local climbers who have up to date information.

Loose rock is an ever present danger when climbing. Rocks may be dislodged by the party or by other climbers. Animals and other natural triggers may start a rockfall. The use of helmet to protect against injury not only from falling rock but also from injuries sustained as a result of a fall, is strongly recommended.

If you have any doubts about your ability to conduct yourself safely on rock climbs you should consider engaging a Guide or an Instructor to lead you or instruct you in the techniques required to climb in safety.

There are no warranties, whether expressed or implied, that this guidebook is accurate or that the information contained in it is reliable. There are no warranties of fitness for a particular purpose or that this guidebook is merchantable. Your use of this book indicates your assumption of the risk that it may contain errors and is an acknowledgement of your own sole responsibility for your climbing safety.

GENERAL INFORMATION

WEATHER

Information about the weather and weather forecasts can be obtained in the Meteo office in the Maison de la Montagne in the centre of Chamonix. A twice daily bulletin is posted on a notice board in front of the office. For those who don't understand French a version in English is also posted but is not updated so frequently.

Tourist offices and Guides Bureaux in each area also display daily weather forecasts and general forecasts can be read in daily newspapers.

A recorded weather forecast can be obtained over the telephone. This is usually updated three times daily. Once at 0700 hrs then again at 1000hrs and finally at 1800hrs. The number to ring is **36 68 02 74**. (BEWARE this number does occasionally change without notice!)

Remember that rain and low cloud in the Chamonix valley does not necessarily mean that it is the same elsewhere.

PLACES TO STAY

Tourism is the mainstay business in the whole region and as such it is incredibly well served by campsites, dortoirs and Gites. Basic Hotel accommodation is generally good value and it is possible to have a three bedded room in a Logis de France establishment for as little as 250ff per night for the room.

Dortoirs represent good value too, as do Gites d'Etape. Lists of such establishments can be obtained from local tourist offices or from the French Tourist Office in London.

Campsites abound and outside the busiest periods it should not be a problem to find a site. Wild camping is illegal in all areas. During the busiest part of the summer, August, it is advisable to book campsites in advance.

LOCAL TRANSPORT

For the climbing closest to Chamonix it is possible to use public transport to get to the climbing quite efficiently. Both the buses and the trains are frequent and comparatively inexpensive.

For climbing areas further afield it is more problematical in that numerous changes of trains or buses will be necessary and it will be time consuming. Having established oneself in a particular valley it is a much more straightfoward procedure to get around.

RESCUE

Any rescue conducted in a remote location is undertaken by the PGHM. Such rescues will inevitably involve the use of a helicopter. All rescue is charged for in Europe and you should make sure that you have adequate insurance cover that not only includes rescue but also medical treatment and re-patriation. It is also advisable to have some level of third party cover.

If an emergency occurs on a roadside or communal Ecole d'Escalade, it may well be conducted by the Pompiers of the commune.

Some useful telephone numbers are as follows:

PGHM in Chamonix **50 53 16 89**

Gendarmerie **17 (this number will get the police anywhere in the region)**

Pompiers **18**

Rescue at the Falaise de Porte **50 71 22 01**

Rescue in the Giffre valley **50 34 45 05**

In Switzerland . . .

Police Cantonale **027/22 56 56**

Air Glaciers **027/22 64 64**

Rega **01/47 47 47**

SOME OTHER USEFUL NUMBERS

OFFICE DU TOURISME

Chamonix	50 53 00 24
La Clusaz	50 02 60 92
Samoens	50 34 40 28
Sixt	50 34 49 36
Mieussy	50 43 02 72

BUREAU DES GUIDES

Chamonix	50 53 00 88
Independants Chamonix	50 53 27 05
Argentiere	50 54 00 12
Vallorcine	50 54 60 69
La Clusaz	50 02 60 92
Samoens	50 34 43 12

and for the best selection of the best gear and the friendliest service . . . SPORTS ALPINS Place de Chamonix Sud, CHAMONIX. (English Spoken)

ENVIRONMENTAL CONSIDERATIONS

The whole of the Chamonix valley and its environs is among some of the most spectacular and beautiful mountain scenery in the world. Unlike more remote and inaccessible mountainous regions, Chamonix is within easy grasp of the modern day traveller. As such it is vastly over populated during the holiday seasons. The influx of hordes of visitors is not without devastating impact on the fragile eco systems of the mountains.

Take care wherever you tread and consider carefully any ways in which you might minimise the effects of your visit on the environment. Stick to footpaths wherever they exist and be careful not to leave any litter or evidence of your passing. Do not pick wild flowers or remove vegetation from the cliffs – a small plant clinging tenuously to life on a precipitous cliff may have taken many years to establish its existence. Climb quietly using only minimal shouting to communicate particularly within earshot of habitation. Behave considerately to other climbers and be respectful of the local people.

A number of crags in this guidebook are in nature reserves. The laws and rules relating to conduct in such areas are strict and are implemented to protect the environment in which we climb. Please respect these rules. Continual failure to observe proper care will inevitably destroy the fragility of the flora and fauna and may well result in the facility being taken away.

MAPS

A map is pretty essential to find your way around in addition to the simple maps in this book.

The Michelin map Lyon Chambery Geneve number 74 or number 89 Evian Annecy and Briancon, or IGN Series Red. 1:250 000 Savoie Dauphine 112 is all you need to locate all the roads that lead to the climbing. These cost little and will save you more than that in time and petrol getting lost . . .

For more detailed maps the following will be helpful

FRANCE
IGN 3430 ET – La Clusaz Grand Bornand 1:25 000
IGN 3630 OT – Chamonix 1:25 000
IGN 3530 ET – Samoens Haut-Giffre 1:25 000

SWITZERLAND
Carte Nationale de la Suisse 282 Martigny Barberine-Camonix-Verbier. 1:50 000.
Carte Nationale de la Suisse 272 St Maurice 1:50 000

All these maps are available directly from Cordee.

INTERNATIONAL CLIMBING GRADES

French	UK		USA	UIAA	Australia
1	mod		5.2	1	
2	diff		5.3	2	
3	v.diff		5.4	3	11 12
4	4a		5.5	4	13
	4b		5.6	4+	14 15
5			5.7	5-	16
	4c		5.8	5	17
	5a			5+	18
6a	5b	E1	5.9	6-	19
6a+		E2	5.10a	6	20
6b	5c	E2	5.10b	6+	21
6b+		E3	5.10c	7-	22
6c		E2	5.10d	7	23
6c+	6a		5.11a	7+	24
7a		E4	5.11b	8-	25
7a+		E4	5.11c		26
7b	6b		5.11d	8	27
7b+		E6	5.12a		28
7c		E5	5.12b	8+	
7c+	6c		5.12c	9-	29
8a		E7	5.12d	9	30
8a+		E6	5.13a		31
8b	7a		5.13b	9+	
8b+			5.13c		32
		E8	5.13d	10- 10	
8c	7b	E9	5.14a	10+	

This list of international grading comparisons is done very much with tongue in cheek. I don't think that it would be possible to get a general agreement on such a document – but it certainly provokes discussion.

The UK grades give technical and E grades. The E grade at the top of each box represents the lower end of seriousness at the technical difficulty and the E grade at the bottom of each box represents the upper end.

PICTOGRAPHS USED IN THE GUIDEBOOK

 Approximate driving time from the centre of Chamonix given that there are no hold ups.

 Time it takes to walk to the crag from the carpark.

 High level of sunshine hours.

 Limited hours of sunshine.

 no sunshine.

 Possible to climb during rain showers or even heavy rain.

 Number of quick-draws required. Figure represents the most that are needed – not an average.

Height of lower-offs. If climbing on a single rope you will need double the figure recommended. Figures relate to longest climbs.

 Special considerations to heed relative to parking facilities

 Length of abseil. Figure represents distance apart of rap stations.

 Belay

 Number of pitches before going down or up to get off.

 Guidebook reference and other information sources.

 Sizes of Friends recommended

 Sizes of nuts needed

 Risk of snakebite – usually vipers. There are other poisonous snakes in the region though they are not all commonly seen.

DEFINITIVE GUIDEBOOKS AND OTHER INFORMATION

Each of the crags described in this guide appears in a more definitive text elsewhere. As mentioned previously, it would be quite expensive to buy all of the books.

If you become sufficiently enamoured by the climbing in the region you may wish to purchase some or all of the titles. The following are available at the time of writing

CHAMONIX
Guide des ecoles d'escalade de la vallee de Chamonix. By Francois Burnier and Dominique Potard.
Also includes some information on Barberine.

ARVE VALLEY
Escalades dans la moyenne vallee de l'Arve. Gilles Brunot and Denis Cardot. Includes information on Bargy and Malsaire.

GIFFRE VALLEY
Escalade dans la vallee du Giffre. Published by a collective group called Promo-Grimpe.

FORON
Topo is available at the restaurant just up the road from the parking area.

RISSE VALLEY
Escalade a St Jeoire et dans la vallee du Risse. Club Alpin Francais section St Jeoire. Only available from the tourist office in St Jeoire.

FALAISE DE PORTE
Published privately. Written by Bernard Wietlisbach. Available in the village of Bellevaux at a bar.

ROCHER DES ARAVIS
Published privately. Compiled by Pierre Brousseau and Philippe Gallay. Available at the tourist office in La Clusaz.

SWITZERLAND

Escalades Bas Valais et Chablais. Written by Stephane Borgeaud and Francois Roduit. Available at the shop on the col del de Forclaz and others in Martigny. Includes information on Gietroz.

There is an excellent and inspirational coffee table book entitled La Haute Savoie – Les Nouveaux Calcaire. Written by Claude Gardiewn and Wilfred Colonna. Published by Glenat.

There are lots of other guides to the region in addition to those mentioned above. If you manage to purchase them all not only will you have a unique collection there'll be more cragging than you could do in a lifetime.

Chamonix Valley

MONTENVERS

 Montenvers railway

 2 max

 Morning sun to midday

 10 max

 15 minutes

 Ecoles d'escalades dans le Vallee de Chamonix

 25mts (30mts makes life easier)

 30 mts max

The climbing at Montenvers is not simply unique but is also in a great position overlooking the lower reaches of the Mer de Glace. It catches the sun for most of the day but not in the evenings. It's a great place to climb if the heat in the valley becomes too oppressive.

Take the train up to Montenvers – or walk if you really want to! Initially, follow the path that descends to the Grotte de Glace and the refuges up the Mer de Glace. At a signposted junction take the path that is indicated Chamonix/Le Praz and follow it underneath the little telepherique.

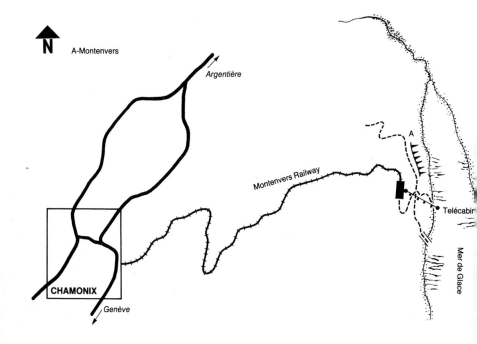

N

A-Montenvers

Argentière

Montenvers Railway

A

Telécabir

Mer de Glace

CHAMONIX

Genève

Occasional faint arrows keep you on course. Finally, near a kind of natural viewpoint on the top of a large boulder, is painted an arrow and the word 'Ecole'. Follow the narrow but well defined path down to the right, as indicated by the arrow, to the top of the cliff. An abseil point is found easily. You'll need a full 50mt rope length to get down in one go but it is possible to do it in two stages.

To reach Sector 3 you must continue along the main path beyond the 'Ecole' rock for about 150mts. A faint path leads in a short distance to a promontory overlooking the cliff. The abseil points are obviously located and the climbs can be reached by two 30mt abseils or one very long stretchy rap!

Sectors 1 & 2 are 'connected' by a cable. The names of most of the climbs are painted at the start of each route.

DESCENT

For getting back to the start of the climbs again, some of the routes have lower-offs that require 50mt of rope if not slightly more. Other than that it is necessary to return, by traversing, to the main abseil descent.

THE CLIMBS

SECTOR 1

1. Roc Dream 6a
2. Dalle Tome 6a
3. Fissure Velue 5+
4. Dimanche a la Plage 6c (7b free)
5. Encorp 6a+
6. Brune Case 6a

SECTOR 2

7. Corto Maltese 5
8. Ciao Tympan 5+
9. Rousse fraise 6a
10. Free 6b
11. Birdy 6c

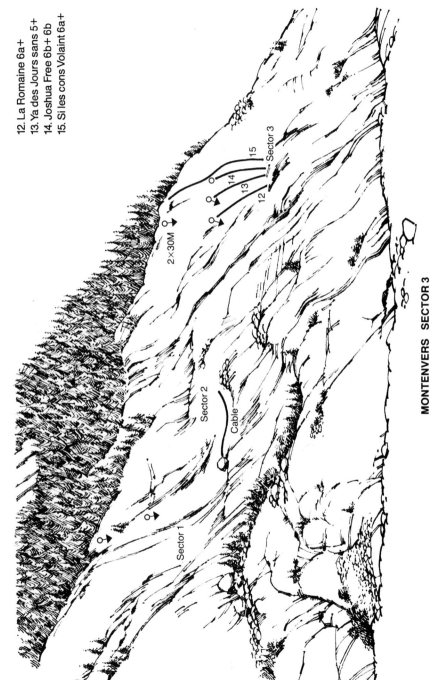

12. La Romaine 6a+
13. Ya des Jours sans 5+
14. Joshua Free 6b+ 6b
15. Si les cons Volaint 6a+

2×30M

Sector 3

Sector 2

Cable

Sector 1

MONTENVERS SECTOR 3

SERVOZ

 15 minutes

 8 max

 Sun in afternoon

 2 max

 25mts

 Ecoles d'escalades dans le Vallee de Chamonix

 20 seconds!

 50 mts

A sunny crag on the outskirts of the village of Servoz. The crag is right next to the road opposite a bar on the D13 Servoz to Chamonix road. Easy parking. The lower reaches of the cliff are at an easy angle and provide straightforward climbing. The upper part is steep, if not overhanging. the climbs are on a sedimentary rock that appears at first, alarmingly loose. However, the rock has been well cleaned and the majority of climbs are solid with enormous holds.

The climbs are very well equipped with large bolts.

DESCENT

Either by abseil, 45mt, or by a track on the left of the crag.

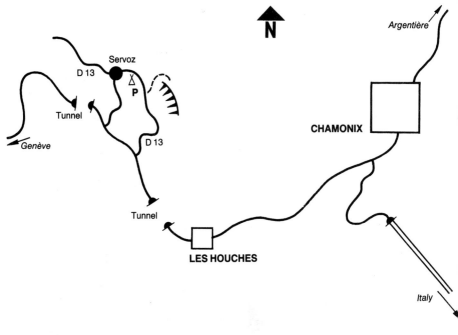

SERVOZ

MONT BLANC

THE CLIMBS

Few of the climbs are named.

1.	5	5.	3+	10.	4
2.	5+	6.	6b	11.	6b
3.	6a+	7	5.5+	12.	6b+
3a.	6c	8.	5.6b	13.	6b+
4.	6b	9.	5.5	14.	6a

Servoz

Servoz

Sallanches Valley

CASCADE DE ARPENAZ

 30 minutes   3 max

 5 minutes   Sun in afternoon

 8 max   25mts

 25mts   Escalades dans le Moyenne Vallee de L'Arve

As you drive down the valley from Chamonix you cannot fail to notice a huge and impressive waterfall cascading over the cliffs just beyond Sallanches. A crag has been developed just to the right of the waterfall that is well worth a visit.

The climbing is mostly at around grade 5 with a few harder problems. There are a couple of three pitch climbs that are worth doing and the climbing has lots of interest – not to mention a cooling spray from the waterfall when the wind blows hard.

Cascade de Arpenaz. The Climbing is to the far right of the photo.

To reach the crag, take the N205 which is the 'old' Sallanches to Cluses road. Shortly after passing underneath the motorway a road leads off right to Luzier. Take this then a left turn at the next crossroads. In less han a kilometre you arrive below the waterfall where there is plenty of parking in a field on the left or, better, further along the rough track. The crag is signposted and is reached in less than 5 minutes from the car. The names of all the climbs are inscribed on elaborate plaques at the start of each route.

DESCENT

All climbs are best descended by lower-off or in the case of the longer climbs by abseil at 25m intervals.

map 10

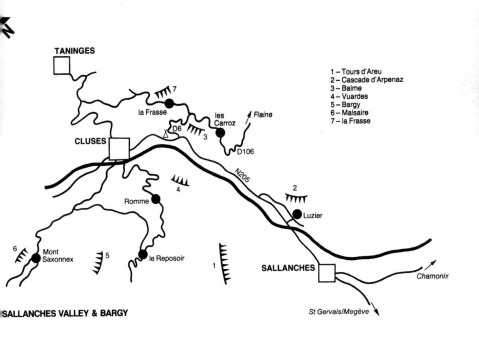

1 – Tours d'Areu
2 – Cascade d'Arpenaz
3 – Balme
4 – Vuardes
5 – Bargy
6 – Maisaire
7 – la Frasse

SALLANCHES VALLEY & BARGY

Cascade de Arpenaz

THE CLIMBS

1. Le matin en Patins 6a
2. Le Intrus 6b
3. Les Farrates 4b
4. L'Opera des P'tits Rats 5b 5b
5. Le Passager Philosophe 6b
6. L'Entremetteuse 5c 5c
7. Shiva 5c

TOURS D'AREU

 40 mins

 6

 1hr to hut then 45 min–1hr

 45 max

 Faces due South

 1–7

 12

 1–2$\frac{1}{2}$

Escalades dans Moyenne
Vallee de L'Arve

These remarkable crags are situated high above the Vallee de l'Arve. They can be viewed most easily from the town of Sallanches. The cliff is naturally divided into five main buttresses. The demarcation between each being large well defined gullies.

The cliffs average some 200 metres in height and the climbs are of high quality. Only three climbs are described but there are some 14 routes altogether to date. The rock is good limestone – compact and rough in places and intricate in others. The setting is superb and there is a tremendous feeling of exposure perched so high above the valley.

The approach to the cliffs, whilst being a shortish drive, is long. A 4 × 4 vehicle makes life considerably easier and provides a good deal of excitement. Most climbers will no doubt prefer to take a more traditional approach by walking in to the Chalets Doran, staying the night and then climbing the next day.

From the centre of Sallanches follow the road that is signposted Burzier. This is a very tortuous and twisting road that gains height rapidly. Shortly after passing through a collection of chalets called Les Houches, the road divides. Take the left fork signposted Telesiege de Burzier. There is ample parking here The Refuge Doran (CAF) is reached in

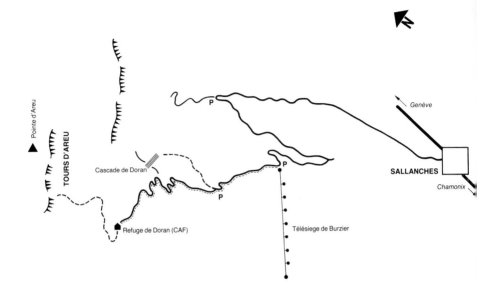

about an hour from here along a very obvious track. A short excursion to the waterfall of Doran is worthwhile. From the refuge, the climbs are reached in 45 mins to 1 hour.

The cliffs face pretty much due south so are in the sun for much of the day. The altitude of around 2000 metres makes a pleasant break from the oppressive valley heat during the hottest days of the summer.

THE CLIMBS

1. Alcotest ED sup 7a is situated on the Premiere Tour. This is perhaps the finest climb on the Areu giving steep wall climbing on rough limestone with plenty of interest. The fourth pitch is the crux though the actual 7a section is fairly short. The start of the climb can be located easily enough on approaching the Premiere Tour. The South-west pillar presents an impressive profile and the line is generally on the left side of the pillar. Start just right of a large obvious cave. The first few metres are somewhat poorly protected but once you reach the overhanging section the bolts begin to appear!

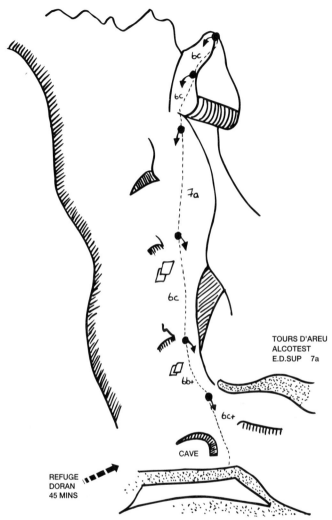

2. Le nuit des loups-garous. ED inf 6c is situated on the Troisieme Tour. The climb begins near the right arete of the buttress and takes the obvious crack line on the face at mid height. The crux of the climb is reserved for the final pitch where a bulging wall tests stamina as well as technique. Much of the rest of the climbing is on superb steep walls. The rock on pitch 2 requires some care. Route finding is fairly straightforward as there are no other climbs to lure you away from the line.

35

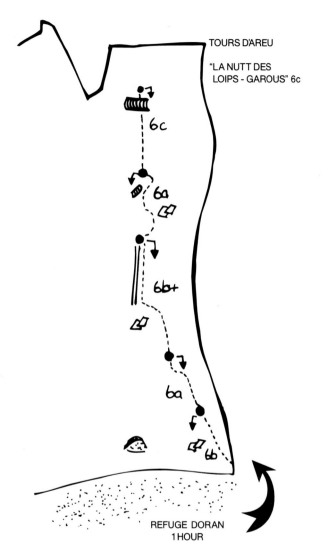

TOURS D'AREU

"LA NUTT DES
LOIPS - GAROUS" 6c

6c

6a

6b+

6a

6b

REFUGE DORAN
1 HOUR

2. Jonothan Livingstone ED inf 6c+ is a worthy climb on the Quatrieme Tour. This takes a line towards the left edge of the buttress up a fairly broad and ill defined arete. The rock is immaculate and the climbing intricate and varied with one very thin and technical key pitch. Route finding is relatively simple but there are other climbs on either side which may be confusing. None of the climbs cross each other however apart from on the penultimate pitch, so once on the climb it is straightforward to follow. The start is located about 15 metres out from the steep corner below a small obvious jutting roof. Above the second, crux, pitch the climb begins to take a very slight diagonal line passing below an obvious crack/chimney line at 3/4 height.

A rack of small to medium wires might be found comforting at times on these routes.

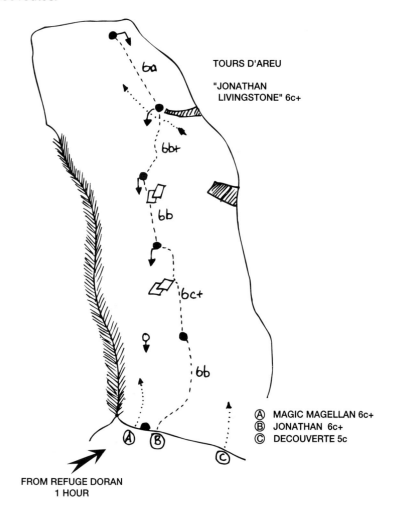

TOURS D'AREU

"JONATHAN
LIVINGSTONE" 6c+

6a

6b+

6b

6c+

6b

Ⓐ   MAGIC MAGELLAN 6c+
Ⓑ   JONATHAN 6c+
Ⓒ   DECOUVERTE 5c

Ⓐ   Ⓑ

Ⓒ

FROM REFUGE DORAN
1 HOUR

DESCENT

All climbs are best descended by abseil. Each is equipped at approximately 40m intervals. The line of descent follows the line of ascent for Alcotest and Le nuit des loups and apart from the final two raps, so does Jonathan Livingstone. The last two raps on that climb go straight down towards the corner from the top of pitch 2.

It is possible, though hardly preferable, to climb to the top of the crag and traverse across left towards the steep broad gully coming down to the Col de la Forclaz.

Tours D'Areu..1. Alcotest 2. Le Nuit des loups - garous
3. Jonothan Livingstone
NOTE: the photos used here to illustrate the cliff were taken in the early spring time. They have been used to show the cliff more clearly . Under snowy conditions such as those seen in the pictures the slopes below the cliffs can be quite dangerous.

LES VUARDES

 45 mins

 30 mins

 12–14

 Sun to Middayish

 Escalades
Moyenne Vallee d L'Arve

 Keep the track clear

 9 walk off

 $2\frac{1}{2}$–$3\frac{1}{2}$ for comfort only

 6–9 for comfort only

The cliff is well positioned above the road from Chamonix to Geneva. Unfortunately it is one of the cliffs that you always strain your neck trying to get a good view of as you're driving down the motorway and almost cause a multiple pile up because you've swerved across the road.

The best view can be had from the N205 near Magland. There are plenty of laybys along the road. The cliff is huge, both in height and extent, and there are many climbs other than the one described here. This particular climb is included for the simple reason that it is a great climb and there is no better introduction to the other routes on the cliff.

The approach to the crag is unusual in that it is from above. The way is quite circuitous and can be difficult to find. There are however a number of landmarks indicated on the route plan and on the photos. A topo of the route is included to ease the route finding whilst on the climb.

Take the road into the town of Cluses and follow signs for Scionzier. Having crossed over the motorway take the road that is signposted to Nancy sur Cluses and then to Romme Pass through the village of

Romme on the road to Reposoir. 150 metres or so along the road a forest track cuts off left and crosses the line of the Winter Teleski. Follow this track which is OK for cars with a reasonably high clearance, for about 2km. You arrive at the road end and a small shed on the right. Park here.

From the car, head pretty much due east. A small ill defined path shows the way. After about 300 metres you should arrive at the top of a broad open couloir cutting the cliff face. Descend this, steeply at times but nowhere horrendous, until you reach the bottom of the couloir. Turn to the left and follow the very foot of the cliff along until you reach a cable. Descend the cable and then go up and along a little further to the foot of the climb. This is an obvious chimney in the right hand side of a huge finger of rock.

DESCENT

Nothing could be simpler – head off north of north west to reach the forest road at the last hairpin of the ascent – About 500 metres.

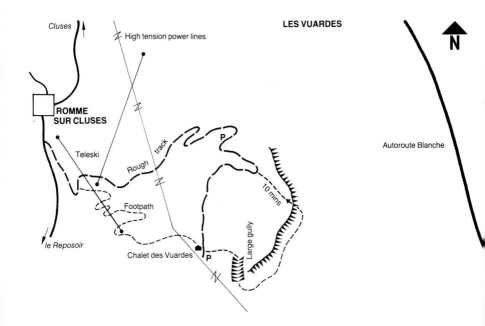

THE CLIMB

Nine pitches of reasonably graded climbing in a brilliant position. The route is exceedingly well equipped but most will draw some comfort from having a few bits of gear other than quick draws. Bigger sizes of nuts and Friends would be most appropriate.

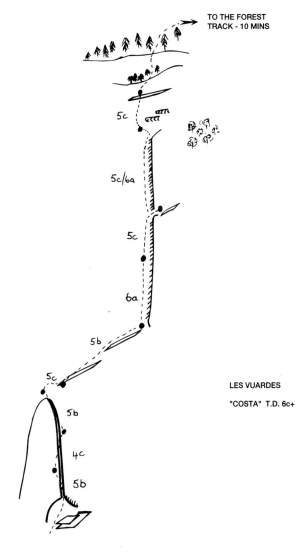

TO THE FOREST
TRACK - 10 MINS

5c

5c/6a

5c

6a

5b

5c

5b

4c

5b

LES VUARDES

"COSTA" T.D. 6c+

Les Vuardes, approach route to Costa (look for the pylon)

BALME

 30 minutes

 50m

 5–15 minutes

 Roulette Russe 9 pitches (rap to Balmette)

 West facing sun from midday

 Vieux au Montagne 6 pitches rap Route

 12 (14 for Realité)

 Punk Not Dead 5 pitches rap route

 Realité non ordinaire 6 pitches walk off

 Escalades Moyenne Vallee d L'Arve

Of the crags described in this guidebook this is one of the most impressive. It has a good concentration of long hard climbs with a 'big' feel about them. The routes on the main part of the cliff yield good quality steep and sustained climbs. Roulette Russe and Realite non Ordinaire are both stunning climbs and memorable outings.

The crag is easily and obviously seen above the road that leads to Flaine from the N205 just a few kilometres before Cluses.

The cliff is characterised by a huge overhang with a right angled corner leading to its left side. Le Vieux de la Montagne is a superb 6 pitch climb taking the pillar to the left of the overhang. To the left of this section there is some broken ground then a much more continuous section of rock which actually overhangs the road. The wall to the right and the obvious crack line is taken by Roulette Russe, a sustained and atmospheric climb with some very hard 7b climbing above the crack.

Realite Non Ordinaire takes a line passing to the right of the obvious roof while further to the right of the main cliff there is another, easier route worthy of attention, Punk Not Dead.

APPROACH

Parking is limited mainly to the bend immediately below the crag. Do not be put off if there are lots of cars – it is also a very popular caving venue. If all spaces are taken you may have to park lower down and there is a path that cuts the zig-zags in the road.

Finding the start of Roulette Russe is easy enough. You must however be careful not to knock down rocks on to the road below.

Reaching the start of Au Vieux de la Montagne is less straightforward. The path is vague. Initially follow the path to the caves for about 100 metres from the parking place. An ill defined track leads back left and up some quite loose but easy scrambling through the vegetation. Keep an eye on the large roof all the time, this is the best indication of where you are in the undergrowth. You should aim for the left hand end of it and you'll come across the broad chimney in the right hand side of a pinnacle. This gives the early part of the climb.

For Realite Non Ordinaire take the caves footpath. This has a very thin cable along the base of the cliff where the path is most exposed.

For Punk not Dead sector follow the marked path along the base of the crag but avoid any obvious ascent. (There is a cable way that lures you to climb up until you reach an electron ladder that, curiously, hangs down the cliff. This is not the way!). Punk not Dead is reached by a short scramble.

DESCENT

All of the routes except Realite non Ordinaire, are equipped to abseil back down though good care should be taken as some of them are very overhanging and one could easily end up hanging in space, unable to regain contact with the rock.

If you have any energy left after Roulette Russe, rap the top two pitches down to the obvious large ledge and do a few routes on Balmette!

It is preferable to walk off from the top of Realite non Ordinaire unless you are fimiliar with any of the abseil descents. The crag of Mortenaz can be reached in about 5–10 minutes and then it is an easy, if quite long, walk back to the parking at the foot of the face.

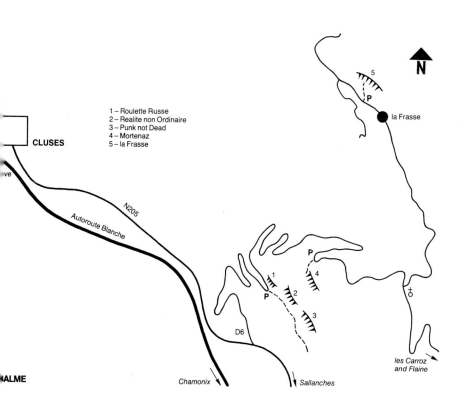

1 – Roulette Russe
2 – Realite non Ordinaire
3 – Punk not Dead
4 – Mortenaz
5 – la Frasse

1. Roulette Russe ED Sup 6b+7b 6c 6a 6c+ 7a+ 7b 6a+
2. Vieux de la Montagne ED 5c+ 6a 6c 6c 6b 6c
3. Realite non Ordinaire ABO inf 6b+ 7b 7a+ 6c 6c 7a
4. Punk not Dead TD sup 6a 6b 6a+ 6a+ 5c

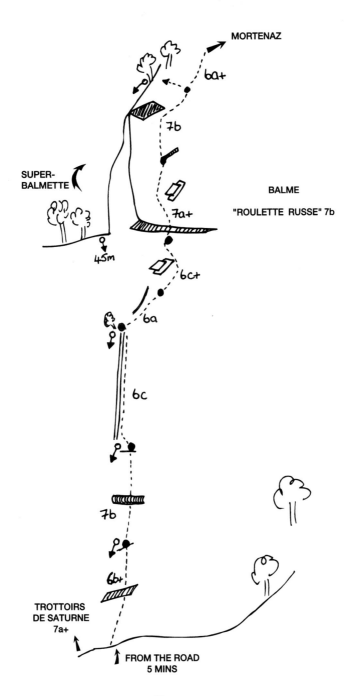

MORTENAZ

6a+

7b

SUPER-
BALMETTE

BALME

"ROULETTE RUSSE" 7b

7a+

45m

6c+

6a

6c

7b

6b+

TROTTOIRS
DE SATURNE
7a+

FROM THE ROAD
5 MINS

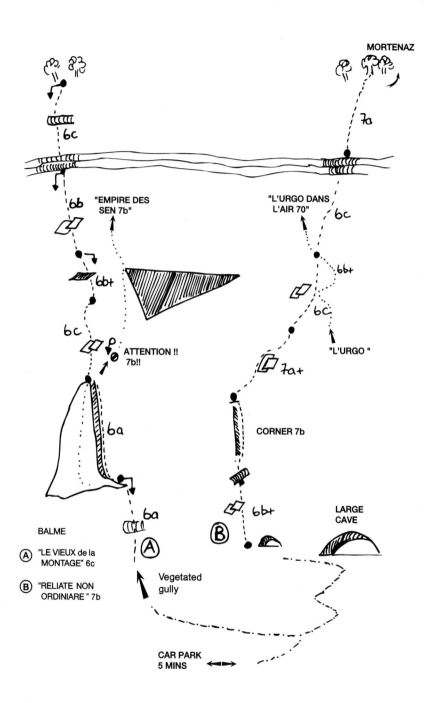

MORTENAZ

7a

6c

6c

"EMPIRE DES
SEN 7b"

6b

"L'URGO DANS
L'AIR 70"

6b+

6c

6b+

6c

"L'URGO "

6c

ATTENTION !!
7b!!

7a+

6a

CORNER 7b

6a

6b+

BALME

Ⓐ "LE VIEUX de la
MONTAGE" 6c

Ⓑ "RELIATE NON
ORDINIARE " 7b

Ⓐ

Ⓑ

LARGE
CAVE

Vegetated
gully

CAR PARK
5 MINS ◄►

48

Balme   1. Roulette Russe
        2. Vieux de la Montange
        3. Realite non Ordinaire

Balme   2. Vieux de la Montange 3. Realite non Ordinaire

Balme   4. Punk not Dead

BALMETTE AND
SUPERBALMETTE

 30 minutes

 10 max

 5–10 minutes

 Mostly 25m–40m rap on Balmette

 Sun from midday

 Roadside

 Escalades
Moyenne Vallee d L'Arve

These two crags are included together as they are both reached from the same parking area.

The climbing here is on steep limestone with very positive holds. The rock is excellent and the situation, perched high above the valley, is superb.

APPROACH

Follow directions as for Balme but continue along the road below the cliff. On arrival at the second switchback further up the road park as soon as you can. A small path cuts horizontally into the trees and both crags are reached in a few minutes.

Balmette is the lower crag and is reached by taking the horizontal path. For Superbalmette take the path that climbs to the left and scramble up a fixed rope to arrive at the crag.

DESCENT

For the longer climbs on Balmette it is necessary to descend by abseil. The shorter ones can be done on lower off with a stretchy 50 metres rope.

Climbs on Superbalmette are much shorter and can all be descended by lowering off.

THE CLIMBS

The climbs on Balmette are not named, but the grades are marked on the rock and the lines are relatively straightforward to follow.
1. 6c
2. 7a. 7b
3. 6c+

The climbs of Superbalmette are slightly obscured by trees in the photo. The crack line of P'tit Loup is obvious and the remainder of the climbs can be worked out from there.

4. P'tit Loup 6c
5. L'Arbre en papier 7c.

Other climbs worthwhile but not shown are:

Polichinel 6b+ just right of route number 4.
Barberousse 6b just to the left of the distinctive vegetated chimney line towards the right hand side of the crag.
Le Vent de la Revolte 7b+ is a line to the left of route 4

MORTENAZ

 30 minutes

 10 max

 10 minutes

 25m for most
30m for longer climbs

 Shaded by trees.
Some sun after midday

 Roadside

 Escalades
Moyenne Vallee d L'Arve

This crag is included for completeness. Many of the climbs are worthwhile, if a little polished, and it is only a short walk from the car.

Development of the climbs has been fairly intense and the climber can be faced with the problem of routes being difficult to link together as many cross and re-cross each other. That said it is nonetheless worth a visit, particularly to climb those routes described.

All the names of the climbs are inscribed at the start and all are equipped with lower offs. Some routes require a 55m rope.

APPROACH

The cliff is reached by continuing along the road from the main cliff of Balme. Continue past Balme for another 5 switchbacks. On the sixth there is a small chalet tucked in the trees and a sign that indicates an 'ecole d'escalade'. Park here and walk along to the crag in about five minutes. The path is well defined and you should not deviate from the most obvious way.

DESCENT

All the climbs are best descended by lower off or by abseil. The longer routes will require a 60 metre rope to lower off from.

NOTE: The crag is surrounded by trees and so it is not possible to photograph it. Locating the climbs is very straightforward as the name of the climb is inscribed at the start. The following list are routes of quality and are described from left to right as you approach the cliff.

THE CLIMBS

1. Manoilles 5c
2. French can can 6a
3. Pipou 6b+ 6b
4. Ca fume la pipe 6c
5. Miniminette 6b Pitch 2 Garde Fou 6b+
6. Mic Mac 6c
7. Pirlouit 7a+
8. Au Fou 6c 6c+
9. Vingt ans Deja 7a
10 Des sous Chics 7b+

LA FRASSE

 40 mins

 8 max

 2 mins

 Some 25m

 All day

 Max 2x30

 Escalades
Moyenne Vallee d L'Arve

This delightful little climbing area is situated to the north-west of the pretty village of La Frasse. It has a sunny aspect and dries very quickly after rain. Though there is little to satisfy those who climb beyond grade 5, the crag has plenty to offer for those up to that standard and being generally of a low angle, is ideal for beginners.

The left side of the slab is, for some peculiar reason, not equipped for the first 20m or so and the routes to the right are over-equipped! Those on the left attain a height of some 70m. Further right again is an area that has been specifically arranged for beginners.

APPROACH

The crag is reached by taking the road towards Les Carroz and Flaine. On arrival in the village of Araches there is a crossroads in front of the church.

Turn left along the D6 for about 2km and the crag will be found just beyond the village. It is easily seen from the approach to it and is the easy angled looking slab with lots of flutings. There is plenty of parking just below the crag.

DESCENT

For the majority of climbs it is better to descend by abseil down the route of ascent and they are well equipped for this. Otherwise, a descent can be made to the right of the crag as you face it.

THE CLIMBS

These are very easy to follow and are nowhere much more difficult than 5b/c. The majority are about grade 4.

Bargy & Aravis

MALSAIRE

 40 Min

 on private land in a meadow Be respectful

 5 Mins

 Escalades Moyenne Vallee de'LArve

 Quickdraws 8 - 10

 South facing but some climbs shaded by trees

 30mts max Most 25m

 Possible to climb below the 'wave' during showers

For the ultimate 'pump out' pay this crag a visit! Though there are a number of climbs around the 6b grade, the majority are much harder, the most difficult being Nuit Blanche 8b. The crag is characterised by a huge and grossly bulging wave-like formation at its right hand end. The slabs below look quite easy angled by comparison but don't be misled.

To the left of the 'wave' the crag becomes rather more amenable and has some excellent technical test pieces.

The rock is brilliant with very small but very sharp holds and some amazing pockets. Furthermore the bolts are of the big fat variety.

For those seeking some respite from the heat of the sun this crag has an advantage over some others in that it is very shady, either by trees or by the huge bulging wall that runs along the top! Nonetheless, it does get very hot during the height of summer. It is possible to climb below the 'wave' during rain.

Despite the fact that the majority of climbs are in the upper grades it is still worth a visit for the quality 6b climbs that exist.

The names of all the climbs are painted at the start of each route. The pitches over the 'wave' have separate names.

A 60 metre rope is recommended.

APPROACH

Parking is possible in the centre of the village. Alternatively take the Bonneville road from the centre and look out for a small right turn marked 'Malsaire Le Homme Fleuri'. This approach to the crag from the village feels rather as if you are driving into someones private driveway. Persevere because it soon leads to a rough track and meadows. Parking is only possible in the meadow opposite the chalet at the track end. From here a well defined path leads into the forest and up to the crag.

It is very difficult to photograph the crag as it is well hidden from all angles. The routes are easy enough to identify by the name inscribed at the start. The following list outlines the best routes, with their grades, from right to left as the crag is approached.

THE CLIMBS

1. Le Seigneur des Anneaux 6b+
2. Coup Tartine 7a
3. Sexuelle deflagaration 6c+
4. Sombres heros 6c+
5. Nuit Blanche 7a+
6. A L'Usine de Eugene 6c
7. La BD 6a+
8. La Chouette 6a
9. Cuculatiforme 7a

Second pitches on the wave
10. Jardin de Balatta 7b
11. Voltige d'Oree 7b
12. Coup Tartine 8a+
13. Nuit Blanche 8b
14. Mister Swing 7c

PETIT BARGY

 45 Min

 Escalades Moyenne Vallee de'LArve

 1 Hour (30 Min with chair lift)

 NW facing some sun in Summer afternoons

 1 Large car park by Chair lift

 7 Max Abseil Route

 Quickdraws 12

 Escalades Moyenne Vallee de'LArve

Note:- Voie Des Trous is a walk off

 50 mts Med-large Mixture might be found useful for 'TROUS'

The Bargy has some of the most enjoyable climbing experiences on of-fer in this guidebook. It can definitely be classed as a mountain experi-ence with all the trappings of that sort of climbing and yet it is most accessible, has a friendly feel about it and is set above an almost, were it not for the hordes of visitors, idyllic lake. It is well worth sampling the unique ambiance of the cirque by bivvying on the shores of the lake either before or after doing a climb. (Strictly speaking this is not per-mitted but it does seem to be tolerated).

It is a popular venue for climbers, particularly at the weekend when the chairlift is operating, and owing to the nature of the cliff, helmets are re-commended wear.

The classic of the crag, the Voie des Trous, is an easy proposition in a marvellous setting. The slabs to the left, which are equipped to abseil from the ledge, offer some very exciting climbing and some thoroughly enjoyable outings. Beware though, that the first ascentionists must have been slab climbing demons because a few of the climbs, particularly the Direct du Lac are very thin . . .

The crag doesn't get very much sun until the latter part of the day and even during the summer months can be very chilly.

APPROACH

From Cluses, take the road to Mont Saxonnex. From the centre of the village follow the road that is sign posted Morsulaz and a chairlift. This lift runs at weekends and during busy holiday periods in the summer. The few francs it costs to take the chair save you about an hours walk to the Lac Benit. From the Lac skirt around the northern shore to pick up a small but distinct track leading up hill and SE towards the cliff.

On approaching the cliff it becomes apparent that the climbs begin on a terrace about 50m up. This can be reached by climbing the obvious small gully (exposed to stonefall) or by traversing out left then back right to scramble up to the terrace.

Helmets are strongly recommended – there is much loose rock around and not all of it is dislodged by climbers . . .

DESCENT

For the Voie des Trous you must carry on to the very top of the cliff and come down the broad open scree to the right of the crag.
For the climbs on the main slab it if preferable to descend by abseil. This is complex in that there are a number of possibilities. There are chains and bits of tat all over the slab. A good line is to descend from the middle of the ledge below the overhang to the right of the finish of Hauteclaire and to pick up the descent line of Direct du lac. The latter climb actually continues to the top of the crag via easy slabs and then the same descent as the Voie des Trous can be used. The climbing beyond the point indicated on the photo is somewhat scrappy and devious.

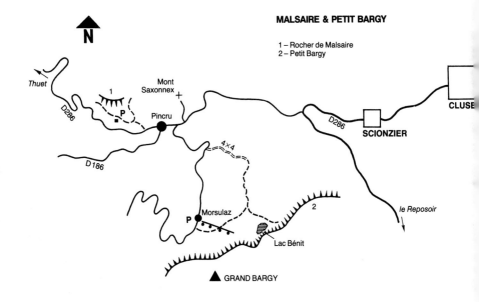

MALSAIRE & PETIT BARGY

1 – Rocher de Malsaire
2 – Petit Bargy

THE CLIMBS

Climbs are very close together on the main slab and it is easy to lose the route. Haute Claire bounds the slab on its left hand side. Direct du Lac takes the obvious left to right slanting break in the middle of the face. All the other routes on the crag fit in around somehow and it is very easy to be lured off route. Beware – the 6b sections are awesome . . .!

1. Haute Claire 4b 5c 5c 5a 6a 6a 5b
2. Direct du lac 5c 6a+ 4c 6b+ 6a
3. Voie des Trous grade 4

Petit Bargy,   Slab area

Voie du Nez (4c max)

Voie des Trous

ie des Trous | 4b | 4c | 5b | 5b | 3b | 3b | 3b

oie du Nez (4c max)

ROCHER DES ARAVIS

 1 hour+

 15 max 10 average

 10 mins

 30 mts preferable

 Sun from midday

 2 max

 Guidebook - Rocher des Aravis

By it's shortest approach from Chamonix, this crag is right at the one hour limit – during the busy tourist season you should leave quite early.

By taking the route through Megeve over the col des Aravis and returning via Col de la Columbiere to Cluses the you will pass through some of the most beautiful pre-alp countryside, where myriad coloured meadows are set against a backdrop of splendid alpine scenery dominated by Mont Blanc.

The climbing is particularly well developed and all bolts and lower offs are in excellent condition. The crag has a variety of climbs of all grades with a particularly good selection of 5's and F6a/6b's. Altogether there are about a hundred climbs of which at least two thirds are worthwhile. Those listed here are but a tasty morsel . . . The excellent guide to the crag is available in the tourist office in La Clusaz.

The crag faces south to south-east and can get very hot during the height of summer. It is a particularly pretty place to climb during the autumn months when the valley floors are enshrouded in inversion mists and the hills remain crystal sharp and clear.

APPROACH

From the Col des Aravis drop down towards La Clusaz and within a kilometre or so the crag comes into view down and to the right of the road.
Parking is in a small disused quarry by the side of the road and on a level
with the crag. The walk in is very short.

If approaching from La Clusaz the crag comes into view as soon as the
road begins to climb more steeply to the Col des Aravis.

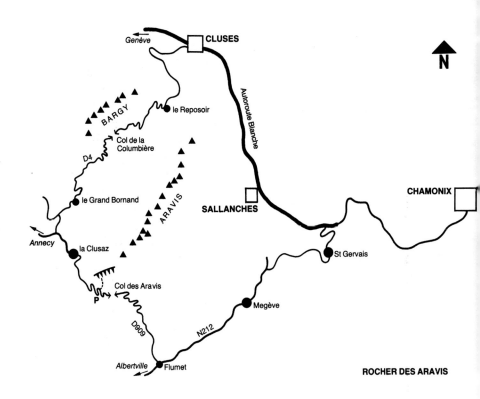

ROCHER DES ARAVIS

Rocher des Aravis,   left side

69

DESCENT

All the climbs are equipped to lower off or, as in the case of the longer routes to abseil. The abseils are no more than 45 metres in length from top to bottom and there are nearly always intermediate rap pointsl. **A 60-metre rope will be found very useful for some of the one pitch climbs.**

THE CLIMBS

The names of all the climbs are inscribed at the start.

1. Un Amour un Passion 7c
2. Le Troisieme Monde 6a 7a+
2a. Le Traverse du Desert 7b+
3. Le Bal des Fous 6b
4. Les Illusions Perdues 6a 6c+
4a. Ballade au bout du Monde 7b
5. Les Quatre Vents 6a+ 6a
6. Desequilbre Fatal 6b 6a+
7. La Recherche du Temps Perdue 6c 6c
8. Solitude Abyssale 6b
9. L'Epee de Damocles 7b+
10. Le Funambule suicidaire 7b+
11. Les Doights de Porcelain 7c
12. Les Quarantiemes Jaunissants 6b
13. Le Grand Toit 8a
14. Le Soleil des Loups 7a+ 7a
15. Autoroute Sauvage 6a+ 6a+

Rocher des Aravis,   right side

Giffre Valley

CHAPELLE SAINT GRAS

 45 Mins-1hour

 10max

 20 Mins to furthest crag

 25 mts some 30 mts

 Most of the day Warm on sunny winter days

 2 max

 Escalades dans la Vallee du Giffre

 50 mts

This is one of the most enjoyable places to climb in the whole region. The selection of climbs in the range 5 to 6c/7a is unrivalled and the setting is glorious.

The crag extends westward from a small chapel which is perched conspicuously on a sylvan hillside a few kilometres west of Tanninges and a little before the village of Mieussy.

Le Recherche du Temps Perdu 6b, Rocher des Aravis

Facing south and in the sun all day, it is preferable to climb early mornings or evenings when the climbs can be enjoyed to their utmost. Even during the depths of winter it is a warm and welcoming place to climb, provided the sun is shining of course.

The cliff extends for almost a kilometre and though to date not all the crags have been developed there is no doubt that it is one of the most significant in the region.

APPROACH

Soon after sighting the chapel from the D907 a narrow and twisty road leads rightwards and one arrives, eventually, at a parking spot some 100 metres from the chapel. From the car park take the track and follow it past the chapel for a further 30 or so metres. A dirt path leads steeply to the right and one soon arrives at the first section. The most significant, and perhaps famous, route here is Les Anges sont aux Bagne (the Angels are in gaol). Some metres further along is a short but worthwhile section with routes such as Vite Fait and Bip Bip. The next section which is diagonally uphill from Bip Bip, provides a concentration of quality climbs from 6a to 6b+ and one classic 5c, Votre Corps Aussi.

For other sections return to the foot of Bip Bip and take a narrow path which gradually gains height along the foot of the cliff. After about 100 metres the next section is seen through the trees. Here the classics are Coucou Cherie 6c 6c and Blues des Cluses 5c6b.

Further along the narrow path one arrives at the section known as F'mur. This provides some quality climbing up to 7a.

About 100 metres further up the path is the most recently developed area and one that hosts some first rate climbs. The classic groove line is Libre Opposition a technical 6c+ offering superb climbing. A few metres left is an obvious cave at about 20 metres height – this contains a very large nest but fortunately not so large bird! The climb to left of the cave is a very worthwhile three star route called Clair de Lune 6a.

Without exception all the routes have the name marked at the start of the climb.

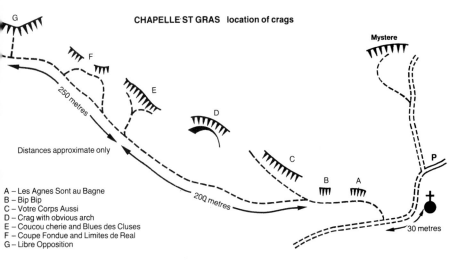

CHAPELLE ST GRAS location of crags

Distances approximate only

A – Les Agnes Sont au Bagne
B – Bip Bip
C – Votre Corps Aussi
D – Crag with obvious arch
E – Coucou cherie and Blues des Cluses
F – Coupe Fondue and Limites de Real
G – Libre Opposition

DESCENT

All the routes are equipped for lower off descent. The 2 pitch climbs though, will require two rappels to reach the ground unless you are climbing on double 9mm ropes.

THE CLIMBS

The climbing is most conveniently split up into sections. Each section is delineated by a clear break in the crag. Unfortunately none of this is obvious from anywhere other than way across the valley.

Chapelle Saint Gras,   Sector A viewed from the approach

SECTOR A

This includes the crag that is visible from the car park and les Agnes

sont au Bagne. The higher buttress is reached in about 10 mins from the car park. Climbs are from right to left.
1. Le Fantasie 6b
2. Badaboks 5c
3. Mystere 6a (you'll soon discover why)

The next climb is approached as for the main crag. See description on page 74. The name and the situation of the climb are immediately obvious to all who have seen the poster!
4. Les Agnes sont au Bagnes 7b

SECTOR B

Bip Bip 6a

SECTOR C

This section is not easily seen from any viewpoint except the air! The climbs are well indicated and the following are worthwhile. Climbs are described from right left.
5. Votre Corps aussi 5c
6. Votre ame nous interesse 6a
7. La dent creuse 6b
8. Takatitakite 6b
9. Manuella 6b+
10. En Catamini 6b+

SECTOR D

Crag with large arch - no climbs included here

SECTOR E

This provides the longest and arguably the best climbs. The climbs are described from right to left. Climb number 11 begins on the left hand side of a huge cave.

11. Coucou Cherie 6c 6c
12. Teuton tetu 7a 7b
13. Itineraire d'un enfant gate 7a+ 7a
14. Les blues de cluse 5c 6b
15. Sysiphie dubitatif 6b+ 6b+

Return to the main path and continue passing below another climbing area Section F, then on beyond for 100 metres to

SECTOR G

The first climb, up an obvious corner is
16. Libre opposition 6c

around on the left are two good climbs to the left of the 'big bird cave'
17. On a marche sur la lune 6a
18. Boulevard des couennes 6b

LE ROC DU SUET

 45 Mins

 12

 5 Mins

 30 metres preferable

 Most of the day

 Stays dry during light rain

 Do not block driveway

 Escalades dans la Vallee du Giffre

There are no climbs on this crag below the grade 6b+. For those with arms like Schwarzneggar, legs like Twiggy and a penchant for the very steep . . . it's a paradise.

This crag is reached from the same approach road as for Chapelle St Gras. Facing SW it has the advantage of catching the late sun and can often be a very good place to climb on sunny winter days.

The crag is so steep that it is often possible to climb whilst it's raining. There are seepage lines after prolonged rain but many of the climbs dry relatively quickly.

APPROACH

Follow the same approach as for Chapelle St Gras. After turning off the D907 on to the little lane go up past two switchbacks in the road. At the third a small track goes off right and is signposted Les Briffes. Park almost immediately. *Do not drive further down the track as it is a private road.* Walk along the track which soon turns into a footpath and leads to the crag in about 10 minutes.

DESCENT

Without exception, all the routes are equipped to lower off. A 55 metre rope would be very useful on some of the routes.

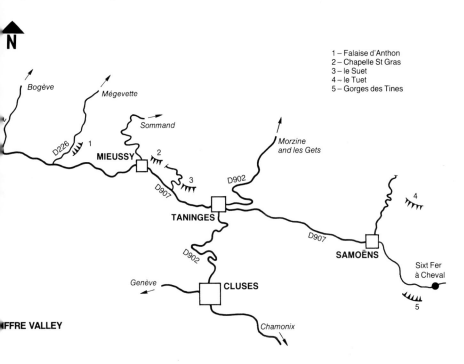

1 – Falaise d'Anthon
2 – Chapelle St Gras
3 – le Suet
4 – le Tuet
5 – Gorges des Tines

Le Roc du Suet

THE CLIMBS

The name of each climb is inscribed at the start.

1. Emoi emoi et moi 7c
2. A vos suets 7b/c
3. Une colonne a la lune 7b
4. Question d'equilibre 7b
5. Royaume de Siam 7b+
6. Humour noir 8a
7. Pouding story 6c+

routes 3 & 4 are obscured in the photo by a tree!

FALAISE D'ANTHON

 50 Mins

 Escalades dans la Vallee du Giffre

 5 secs

 8 max

 Sunny from just before midday faces west

 25m

Situated immediately above the road, this fine crag offers a range of grades to suit most abilities and aspirations. It is very well equipped and most of the climbs can be done with a 50m rope. The cliff dries very fast after even the most heavy rain but watch out for large pockets that hold water for quite some time . . .!

APPROACH

The cliff is approached by taking the road, D907, from Tanninges to Annemasse. Some 2km after passing through the village of Mieussy you turn right along the D226. This is signposted Megevette. After a little more than 1km you arrive at the crag which is situated opposite a small lake – swimming is *not* allowed.

Park at the lake for all the climbing or, if you feel really lazy drive a hundred mts up the road for sectors 3 & 4 described.

The climbing is most easily split into 4 sectors, sector 1&2 being those that are reached first on the approach road described. All the climbs, except for more recent ones and 'projects' have the name inscribed at the start.

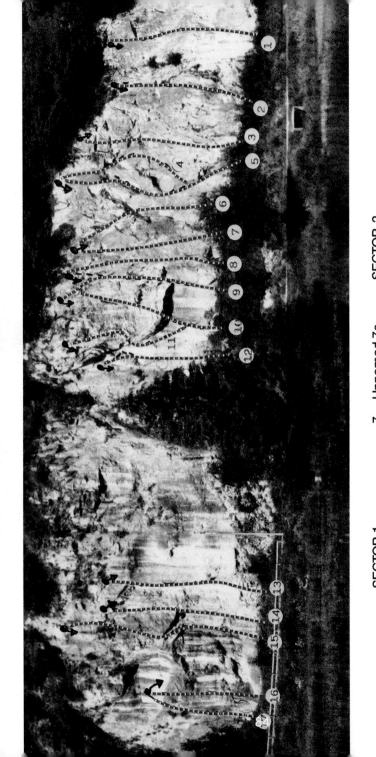

SECTOR 1
1. Vertige 6a+
2. La voie de la arbere 5c
3. Asterix 6b
4/5. Les grillons 6a/6a+
6. Leo et les bas 6b

7. Unnamed 7c
8. Potion magique 6c
9. Bib 6b+
10. Le toit 7b
11. L'assiette
12. Vite fait 6b

SECTOR 2
13. Hugo 7b+
14. Panaoramix 7a
15. Kanaky 7a
16. Bicounet
17. Vert clair 7c

DESCENT

Without exception all climbs are equipped with lower-offs. A 55mt rope will be found useful for some of the longer climbs.

SECTOR 3
18. La goutiere 5b
19. Viol de corbeau 6c
20 Electrochoc 5c
21 Turbostyle 6a

SECTOR 4
The first two climbs are hidden behind the tree in the photo.

22. Le grands tetras 8a+
23. Reve d'o 6b

24. Cramps 6b+
25. Voie X 6b
26. Ya bon le soleil 5b

GORGES DES TINES

 50 Mins

 10 max

 5 Mins

 25m

 Hardly gets the sun

 Possible to climb on main crag during showers

 4 max

 Escalades dans la Vallee du Giffre

 max 45m

This crag is well situated in a particularly attractive valley. The resort of Samoens, a pretty alpine village with good tourist facilities, is only a few kilometres away.

There is a wide variety of climbing from easy slab routes to steep and technical. It has the advantage, during the hot days of summer, that it remains in the shade for much of the day.

The main crag is most easily split into two sections. Both are separated by an obvious cave/arch feature at the base of the crag. The climbs to the right offer superb steep technical climbing on brilliant rock whilst the longer climbs on the left are sustained throughout their length.

The 'ecole' area of slabs yields many possibilities at around grade 5/6 – the only propblem is picking a time to climb when it's not inundated with hordes of people.

Gorges des Tines,   the slab

APPROACH

Take the D907 to Samoens. Continue along the same road, it is sign-posted Croix de Fer. Immediately after Samoens the road is very straight and flat. It then climbs a little through a narrow valley and around a long bend. A large parking area is soon reached. The track to the crag goes across a bridge over a narrow gorge and is signposted.

If you'd like to get a look at the crag beforehand, drive further along beyond the parking place and you get an excellent view.

DESCENT

For the slab routes one can either lower off or walk down to the left hand side.

For climbs on the right of the main cliff either lower off or abseil from the last belay on the two pitch routes.

4'eme Dimension is equipped to abseil down the line of ascent. 30 metres should be sufficient to reach each belay.

Savoie Fer is best descended by abseil. This particular climb is unusual in that it is probably the only climb in this guidebook first ascended by a British climber —Jon de Montjoye. The first rap off the top is about 15 metres and the second 20 metres. The third is directly to the ground in 40/45 metres. It is not possible to regain the first belay stance of the ascent.

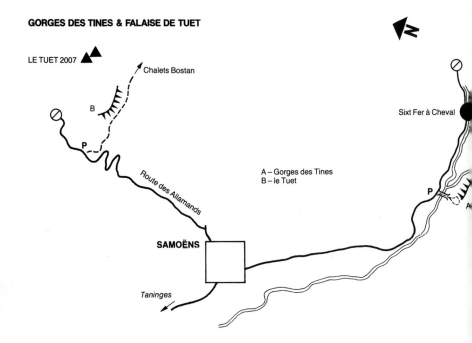

LE TUET 2007

Chalets Bostan

B

Sixt Fer à Cheval

P

Route des Allamands

A – Gorges des Tines
B – le Tuet

SAMOËNS

P

Taninges

THE CLIMBS

The climbs on the slab are all around grade 5 or 6. So many variations are possible that it is best left to individual choice.

Climbs on the main crag are best described from right to left as approached.
1. Ici mieux qu'a cote 6c 7b
2. Quo vadis 7c+
3. Dolby street 6c
4. Les delice de tentation 7b 7b+
5. Terreur aveugle 7a+
6. Victor le nettoyer
7. Savoie Fer 7b+ 7a+ 7b+ 7b
8. 4'eme Dimension 7b+ 6c 6c 5+

Gorges des Tines   8. 4' Eme Dimension   7. Savoie Fer
                    4. Les Delice de la Tentation

Gorges des Tines,   right of cave

Falaise de Tuet

 1 hour

 Lower tiers stay dry for ages during showers

 30 Mins

 10 max

 Much of the day but shady on lower tiers

 25mts

 Escalades dans la Vallee du Giffre

 max 45 mts

Situated in a pretty cul de sac valley not far from the all year resort of Samoens, this crag offers a few surprises – both pleasant and horrendous.

A more diverse climbing area would be difficult to find anywhere; on the one hand are pleasant slabs, open and amenable, of unusually structured limestone and, lurking below in the trees like some devil incarnate are gruesome, yet masochistically enjoyable, climbs to test the strongest arms.

It is a sunny crag that takes little seepage and so dries fairly quickly after rain. The lower walls, protected as they are by themselves, offer opportunities to climb even during rain.

Beware of some of the grades of the easier climbs on the lower crags particularly the grade 5's . . .

The upper slabs have a number of climbs that are not equipped with bolts. Unfortunately the compact nature of the rock does not readily lend itself to nut or Friend protection.

The names of the routes are inscribed at the starts.

APPROACH

From Samöens take an obscure road signposted la Route des Allemand. This road takes the obvious deep valley to the north of Samoens. Go along the road to where it begins to ascend in steep switchbacks. About 500 metres beyond the last switchback is a large clearing in the forest either side of the road. Park here. The crag is signposted and is reached along a pleasant track that traverses a steep hilside, in about 30 minutes.

There are four sections to the crag. The first three are hidden among trees and cannot really be seen until directly below them. The first section is identified by an easy angled slab on its left. Once located, the remaining sections are easy to find as they simply run parallel with and above, the footpath.

The slabs, which attain a maximum length of a little more than 100 metres, are at the far end of the overhanging walls.

DESCENT

All the climbs on the first three sections are descended by lower off. Some of them require a 55 metre rope. It is possible to belay at the top of the climbs as most of them finish on good ledges or easy ground.

For climbs on the main slab area descend by abseil. There are many options of line to choose. It is possible to go down the line of ascent but probably better to mix and match a little. It is also possible to walk off the top of the crag down to the left as you face out. The way is indicated by paint marks.

THE CLIMBS

Routes on the three lower sections are described from left to right as each is approached. The crags are totally obscurred by the trees and it is impossible to take pictures of them. Each climb however, is very obvious and has its name inscribed at the start.

The following are recommended
1. Tete de Lard 6a   3. Assimbonanga 7a+
2. Indonesia 7a   4. Madame la baronne 6c

Le Tuet,   the routes on the slabs

Just around to the right is a short problem wall the first two being 7a+ and 6c+ respectively.

5. Blance Fesse et les 7 mains 6b/c depending on which exit is taken. The most direct is the better
6. L'esprit s'amuse 5b (more like 6b!)
7. Marsupillami 7a+
8. Orejona 7b
9. Naufrage celeste 7b+
10. Seigneur et creatures 7b

THE SLABS

The first two climbs on the slabs are best begun by a common start. There are two possibilities just to the right of route 10. One is 5c and the other 5b. The climbs then split up and go their own way once on the slab proper.

1. Vieux Allamands 5b/c 6b+ 4c 5c 5
2. La Vierge 5b/c 4c 5c 5c

The next two begin somewhat further to the right below an obvious chimney line.

3. Voie Lactee 4 5c 5c 4
4. Galadrielle 4 6a 6a

FORON

 Can Climb during showers

 10-15 mins

 8 max

 Watch for vipers !

 25 mts

 Most of the day

 1 hour plus

 topo at restaurant below crag

This 'craglet', which packs a mighty punch, lies a little bit beyond the one hour limit imposed in selecting the crags. It is included entirely on merit and justifiably so. There are few who have not come away mightily impressed by the experience!

The crag is most aptly described as "grossly overhanging" and offers climbing only to those with very strong arms. All the climbs are F6c or harder, very well equipped and brilliant fun.

All of the climbs are well worth doing even though they are incredibly close together. The selection on offer here is fully representative of the grades and from these it is a simple matter to work out where the others go.

It is a sunny crag throughout the day, remains fairly dry during rain and dries out quite quickly when the rain stops, though you need to look out for seepage lines.

Pay special attention to the risk of snakebite. The rocks around the base of the crag are a favourite basking ground for vipers!

APPROACH

From Tanninges take the D902, signposted Les Gets and Morzine. A few kilometres along the road there is a junction signposted Praz de Lys. Take this road. After 1 kilometre turn off down a narrow road to the right. It is signposted Col de L'Encrenaz. (There is a water trough right on the turn). Follow this road, the D328, through some marvellous scenery until the road begins to climb sharply to the col. Park at the foot of the hill or drive a little further to the restaurant and park. The crag is very obvious and is reached from the lower parking place in about 15 minutes steep walking.

DESCENT

All the climbs are equipped to lower off.

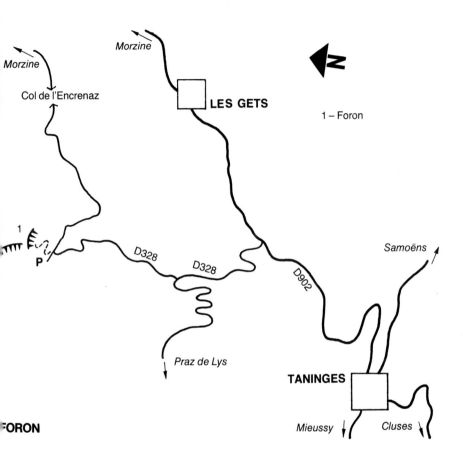

THE CLIMBS

Climbs are described from right to left as you approach the crag. The first climbs are on the front face behind the tree. The names of each climb are clearly marked at the start and are easy to follow.

1. Foron 7a
2. Le voleur de Baghdad 7a
3. Amour defunte 7b

The next climbs are around on the even more overhanging face.

4. Baton de Berger 6c
5. La vista 7a+
6. L'ascenseur 7a
7. Expresso 7a
8. Le Comte des Dinos 7b+

Foron,   viewed from the car park

Valley du Risse

POUILLY

 45 Mins

 10max

 2 Mins

 25 mts OK but 30mt better

 Very sunny

 3 max

 Escalades a St Jeoire et la Vallee du Risse

Pronounced 'poohey' with a French accent, this crag is only a few kilometres down the road from Chapelle St Gras and Anthon and is on the way to Bellosset. It is well worth a visit either in it's own right or as part of a day out visiting the other crags nearby.

The very smooth looking slab as seen from the road provides a number of very good technical climbs some of which require great tenacity. The continuation wall around to the right has a very good selection of climbs at F6b and above.

This crag is the French equivalent of Bwlch y Moch at Tremadoc in that it is owned by a national mountaineering body, the Club Alpin Français. Unlike Tremadoc however, they have protected the environment surroung the crag by the judicious use of permanent lower-offs and abseil points . . . and funnily enough no-one seems to mind.

It can get incredibly hot on sunny days in summer and there are some nasty snakes around about.

APPROACH

From the village of Mieussy take the D907 towards Annemasse. After 5 or 6 kilometres turn right into the village of St Jeoire. Take the D26, signposted Megevette and the Col de Jambaz, out of the village and after a couple of kilometres the crag is obvious on the left. Parking is available opposite the crag and the first climbs are reached within a couple of minutes walking.

DESCENT

Without exception all the routes are equipped to lower off or, in the case of the longer routes, to abseil. A 60 metre rope is useful for climbs on the right wall though it is also possible to walk off.

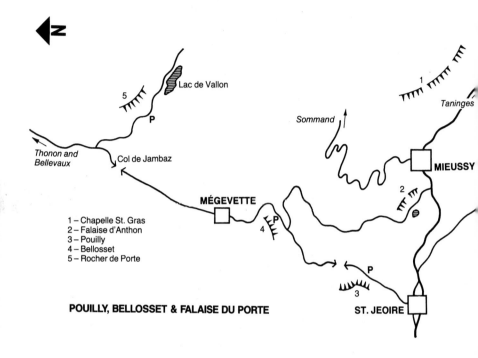

Lac de Vallon

5

P

Thonon and
Bellevaux

Col de Jambaz

Sommand

Taninges

1

MIEUSSY

2

MÉGEVETTE

4

P

P

3

ST. JEOIRE

1 – Chapelle St. Gras
2 – Falaise d'Anthon
3 – Pouilly
4 – Bellosset
5 – Rocher de Porte

POUILLY, BELLOSSET & FALAISE DU PORTE

THE CLIMBS

1. Le diedre de Marseillaise 5c 6a 6b
2. Un Dimanche a la campagne 7b
3. La prolo 6b
4. La reine 6b
5. Tip top 7a
6. La voie ferree 7b (6b with aid)
7. La Fillette 6c

8. Le mur des lamentations 7b
9. La mediane 6c
10. La tangente 6b
11. Illusion 7a
12. Priorite a droite 6c
13. L'instinct du lezard 6c
14. Coco gadgeto verins 7b+

BELLOSSET

 50mins–1hr

 OK during showers.
Boulder during heavy rain.

 5 secs!

 12 max

 Limited roadside
on a bad bend

 30mts recommended.

 Escalade a
St Jeoire dan la Vallee du Risse

This crag, developed in 1992, seems destined to become one of the major crags in the region for hard technical climbing. The rock is compact limestone and is continuously steep and unrelenting. Most of the major lines have now been climbed and there are a dozen routes harder than 7a. There is little below that grade of any note.

There is a rather unusual bouldering area at the left hand end of the crag where some imaginative person has gone to a lot of trouble to bolt on rocks and pebbles from the river bed. Complete anathema to us British folk of course – so I don't suppose you'd be interested in the grades of the problems . . .

APPROACH

From St Jeoire drive along past the crag at Pouilly. Between 1 and 2 kilometres past the village of Onnion (don't forget to buy a string of them . . .) and just before a sharp left hand bend is a small pull in on the left. There is a sign nailed to a tree indicating the crag. Prepare yourself for the shortest walk-in ever – 10 seconds?

DESCENT

All the climbs are equipped to lower off though you will need a 60 metre rope for some of them.

Note: It is not possible to photograph the crag as the trees obscure any view of it. All of the names of the climbs are inscribed at the start and the lines are obvious.

THE CLIMBS

The following climbs are recommended and are described from right to left as the crag is approached.

The first feature is an obvious prow – impressive and impending. To the right of the prow is.

1. Madame Emeraude 7b

The next climb begins on the left of the prow and finishes high on the very top of it. The figure in the photo below is at the start off the following route.

2. Peu ou Proue 7c

The next three climbs are very appealing . . .

3. Les bello balcons 7b+
4. Mon ame le science 8a
5. Mon ombre voler 7c+

Next is

6. Ingen adgang 7a+
7. L'excuse journalaire 7b

Left again, just before the 'radical cave' is an obvious elegant corner.

8. Un-named 7a+?

Coming out of the cave is

9. Low gravity man 8a.

LE FALAISE du PORTE

 1 hour +

 12 max

 3 mins

 Guidebook
Falaisedu Porte

 Very sunny

 30mts preferable

This is a very extensive crag with something for climbers of all standards. It is situated at the one hour limit imposed on the selection of crags. In favourable conditions it can be reached easily within the hour but summer traffic can be most trying . . . If however, you are visiting Chapelle St Gras or Pouilly it is really only a hop skip and a jump away.

The crag is situated on private land and in order to maintain access a local climbing club was formed to develop the climbs and cultivate favour from land owners. Any further development, which is unlikely anyway, should be done in consultation with the club's officers.

The largest portion of the cliff is the left hand side which comes into view from the approach road. To the right the lower part of the cliff is fairly low angled and abounds with easy climbs and some desperately polished slab routes.

There is an annual climbing fete that takes place here. It is very entertaining and there are climbing competitions open to all. Usually the crag is 'closed' for climbing on such occasions.

APPROACH

Follow the directions as for Bellosset but continue along and over the Col de Jambaz. Soon after crossing the col a sharp right turn is signposted Lac de Vallon. Follow this route, the D236, until you arrive at the crag. It is impossible to drive past the cliff without noticing it on your left . . .

It takes a few minutes only to walk to the crag and the path comes out close to the centre of the crag and climbs around 'Amours de Conchita".

DESCENT

All the single pitch climbs are equipped to lower off, though a 55 metre rope will be found useful on some. All the multi pitch routes are well equipped to abseil off, again a 55 or 60 metre rope will be useful.

If you find yourself at the top of the crag without the means to abseil, there is a very well marked descent path that comes down to the right, as you face it, of the cliff.

THE CLIMBS

The names of all the climbs are inscribed at the start. Trees obscure the starts of all the climbs in the photos but they are very easy to locate.

1. Sheerazade 6b
2. Jardins de Babylon 6a 6a
3. Yang 6c 7a
4. Amadeus 7b+ 7a 7a
5. Fruits de la Passion 6b 7a 6c (1pt aid)
6. Biscotte Febrille 6c+
7. Amours de Conchita 6b
8. Bric a Bras 6a

9. Les Cles du Paradis 6c+ 6c 6b+
10. Rock Star 6c+ 8a
11 Capucin 6b+ 7b+

Switzerland

BARBERINE

 20 Min

 12 max

 15 Mins

 Strictly no parking in the village

 Faces SW gets hot

 45m longest

 Vipers & others

 6 maximum

 Guidebook ref.
Escalades Bas Valais et Chablais

This magnificent crag is dominated by two long routes which begin either side of a huge cleaned slab that offers climbs at a reasonable standard.

Despite the fact that this crag is approached from France it is actually in Switzerland! It is not necessary to cross any border control but in case you need to come down into Switzerland you ought to consider carrying a passport.

The cliff is reached by continuing down the road from Vallorcine towards the Frontiere Suisse. As you drive down the road the crag can be seen on the left. Just before you go around the last bend to the Frontiere a sharp turning left leads to the village of Barberine. Drive on past this turning and about 50 metres further on there is a carpark on the right hand side. **DO NOT PARK IN THE VILLAGE**.

Walk back up the road and turn down towards the village. The path to the crag begins where the road narrows, it feels as if you are going to walk through someones garden, which in fact you do! There are usually two electric fences to pass through, the second just before crossing the river by a rickety bridge. Follow the path for about 100m then turn sharply up the hill left. The crag is reached in about 15 mins from the car.

As you approach the crag there are two very obvious cleaned lines, both beginning above and each to one side of the main lower slab. The left hand line, conspicuous by a huge white slab, is the 'Vipere au Pied' and the right, a much narrower cleaned line, is the 'Ballade au Bout des Combes'. Both climbs are excellent but the 'Vipere' is probably the best. To reach the start of these climbs one can either scramble up the right hand side of the slab or do a climb on the slab itself.

Ballade starts just above and right of the cable that is stretched across the top of the slab. To get to Vipere traverse the cable and at it's end continue along a well worn path marked by blue arrows. There is some scrambling and it is exposed in places. The climb begins at the bottom of the white slab above and behind the base of a huge Meleze (larch) tree

DESCENT

For the climbs on the slab it is best to go down the easy scramble to the right of the cliff. For the climbs that finish on the left hand side or the central part of the slab traverse the cable rightwards to reach the scramble.

For the 'Vipere' it is better to descend the route by abseil. The route is well equipped for this and it can be done in 5×40m abseils to the bottom of the climb. To reach the first abseil traverse left at the top of the final pitch and descend directly to the top of the 6b pitch. From here the route is followed in reverse.

For 'Ballade' abseil back down the final headwall in two stages then take a terrace leading down to the left (facing out) a 30m abseil brings you to an ill defined gully and slabs, be sure to keep the pylon to your left. A 10m

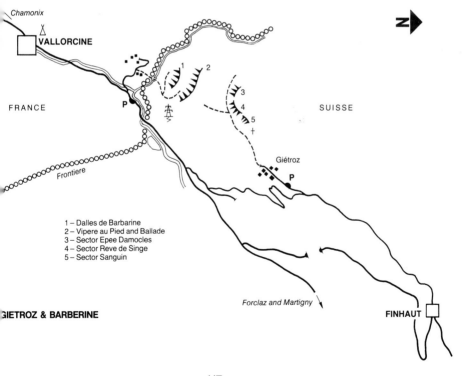

1 – Dalles de Barbarine
2 – Vipere au Pied and Ballade
3 – Sector Epee Damocles
4 – Sector Reve de Singe
5 – Sector Sanguin

GIETROZ & BARBERINE

Africa Flake

abseil further down and more scrambling leads eventually to screes to the right of the main slab. A real adventure!

THE CLIMBS

1. Vipere au Pied 200mts TDsup 5 6a 6a+ 6a+ 6b 6a+
2. Balade au bout des Combes 200mts TDsup 5+ 6a+ 6a 6a 6b 6c
3. No name 5+ 6a+
4. No name 4+ 6a
5. No name 6c

Route number 6 indicated high up in the photo is Guillotine 7a on the Gietroz crags – see next section.

Gietroz

CHATELARD/GIETROZ

 30 Min

 30 mts preferable

 15–30 Mins

 5 max

 Strictly no parking in or beyond the village

 Max 50m

 S.–SE some climbs are enclosed by trees

 Escalades Bas Valais et Chablais

 10–12

 Adders

The climbing at Chatelard is really a continuation of the Barberine cliffs and offers some tremendous climbs, mostly of high standard, on superb rough granite/schist. The area is quite complex being made up of a number of different buttresses and it will certainly take a little time to sort out where the climbs are.

There are a number of ways to approach the crag but perhaps the best, the easiest and most interesting, is to go through the Frontiere and take the first turn left signposted Chatelard Village and Gietroz. After some 200m turn left again and go up a very narrow, very twisty road. Turn left at the next junction to arrive shortly afterwards at the village of Gietroz.

Park 100 metres before a large renovated building on the outskirts of the village. **Do not take your vehicle into the village or beyond**. There is no parking space at all. Walk the few metres into the village and take a narrow road which passes at first between some chalets and continues to a water trough and the most beautiful old alpine chalet.

Carry on along the track to a viewpoint with a bench and a large cross behind. The path from here is indistinct but begins in the corner of the clearing immediately opposite your arrival. This path goes down initially and then leads up into a steeper enclosed gully. This gully is where Reve de Singe is. The name is clearly inscribed at the start. At the top of the gully is an obvious crack. This is the first pitch of Le Piege.

For climbs at the left hand extremety carry on beyond the gully, trending slightly rightwards all the time and following along the bottom of the cliff. You soon come to an obvious clearing and the conspicuous large flake shaped like the continent of Africa.

DESCENT

Without exception, it is better to descend by abseil or lower off from all of the climbs. A 60 metre rope is essential in order to reach the ground on most climbs.

GIETROZ →

Access to crags

Cross

Sector Sanguine ↑

Africa Flake ↓

Reve de Singe

Deep Gully ↑

Return to Barberine ↓

Dalle de Barberine ↓

IMPORTANT NOTE: Some local climbers raised great objection to the inclusion of this crag in the guidebook. Justifiably, not only because it is a great crag to climb on but also because the access hangs in the balance. Please don't jeopardise this access and make sure you keep all vehicles out of the village – it isn't too far to walk.

THE CLIMBS

The climbing is most easily split into two main buttresses. The *Reve de singe* sector and the *Africa flake* sector. The climbs are described from left to right which is the opposite to the way in which they are approached.

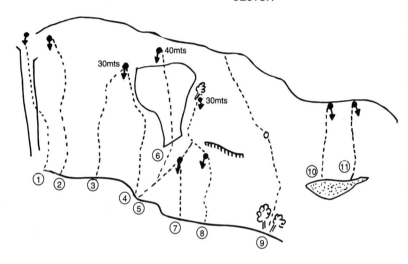

GIETROZ –
'AFRICA FLAKE'
SECTOR

AFRICA FLAKE

1. Luce-ifer 6a
2. L'Epicondylite 7a+
3. Physiotherapie 6c+
4. L'Epee de Damocles 6b+
5. Decouverte 6a
6. Guillotine 7a
7. Black mamba 7b
8. Decouverte Direct 6b
9. La Normale 6a
10. Dalle qui M'aille 7a+
11. Dure de dalle 7a

GIETROZ Sector Reve de Singe & Sanguine

1. Reve de singe 7c+
2. Sortilege 6b+ 6c 6b
3. Petit lune 6b+ 6c 7b

4. Fesse d'huitre 6b 6b+ 6a 6b+
5. Pharon aile 6b+ 6b 6c+
6. Le Mepris 7a+

7. Sanguine 7b
8. Unnamed 6c
9. Le Gaypied 6b 6c

REVE DE SINGE SECTOR

The first climb at the top of the gully previously described is La Piege 6b+ 6b+ and it begins up an obvious crack line about 25mts uphill from Reve de Singe.

1. Reve de singe 7c+ (name is inscribed at the start)
2. Sortilege 6b+ 6c 6b
3. Petit lune 6b+ 6c 7b
4. Fesse d'huitre 6b 6b+ 6a 6b+
5. Pharon aile 6b+ 6b 6c+
6. Le Mepris 7a+
7. Sanguine 7b
8. Unnamed 6c
9. Le Gaypied 6b 6c

DORENAZ

 1 hour plus

 25mts OK

 1 min →20 mins

 Do not park on the grass

 South and west facing

 2–3 1/2 comforting on some climbs

 5 on Tichodrome

 Medium set comforting on some climbs

 12 max

 Guidebook ref. Escalades Bas Valais et Chablais

This collection of crags, situated close to Martigny in Switzerland, is quite often in the rain shadow of the Mont Blanc massif and so during prolonged South Westerly airstreams may prove a good dry alternative.

The climbing is varied and of interest to climbers at all grades, particularly around grade 5 to 6a. The rock is quite different to anything else in this guidebook, being a rough conglomerate with excellent friction and unusually varied climbing.

It is very popular with Swiss schools and climbing courses so you can expect parts of the crag to be very busy at any time.

APPROACH

To reach the crag from Chamonix you must first get to Martigny. From Martigny take the ordinary road out following signs for Evian and Lausanne. Don't be tempted to take the autoroute – you have to go miles down until you can get off it again.

About 4.5 kilometres from Martigny you arrive in the village of Vernayaz. The Gorge du Trient is a significant landmark (and an interesting walk) that is passed just on entering the village. Some 500 metres or more through the village of Vernayaz there is a road off to the right signposted Dorenaz. Take this road which passes over the motorway then the Rhone, to arrive immediately at the crag.

Parking for routes on this sector is obvious. For the other sectors described turn right at the junction immediately after the bridge over the river Rhone.

DESCENT

Most of the climbs on the parking sector are equipped to lower off or to descend by abseil.

For sector Demi Lune it is easier to walk down to the left of the crag.

For Tichodrome walk back from the top of the crag along a grass rake then pick up the descent path for Demi Lune.

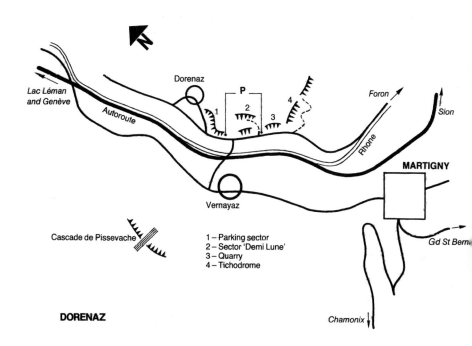

1 – Parking sector
2 – Sector 'Demi Lune'
3 – Quarry
4 – Tichodrome

DORENAZ

THE CLIMBS

Routes are described from left to right as you arrive at the crag.

1. Jackpot 5 5
2. J'embrasse une hombre 6a+
3. Vaudois 6a+ 6b+
4. Carlorigolo 6a 6c
5. Fine fleur 5 6a

This next section is immediately left of the car park.

6. Fissure 5+
7. Azid direct 6b+

This next section is along the road from the car park and is easily seen above a vineyard.

8. Fuillerains 6c 5+
9. Meditation 6b+ 6a
10. In the back 6b+ 5+ 6a+
11. Demi lune 6a 6a+
12. Walking on the moon 6c 6a+
13. Promenade du soir 4+ 5

The next climb is approached by a steep walk from the road, beginning some 100 metres or so along from the quarry.

14. Tichodrome 5+ 4+ 5+ 5+ 6a+

ENGLISH/FRENCH DICTONARY
OF USEFUL CLIMBING TERMS

abseil	rappel
access (time)	acces (temps d'approche)
airy	aerienne / arién
arete	arête
arrow	flêche
ascend	monter
bad	mauvais
barn	grange
belay	relais
bend	lacet
best	meilleurs
bolt	spit, goujon, scellement
boulder (problem)	bloc (pas de bloc)
bulge	bombé
cablecar	télépherique
car	voîture
careful	prudence
cave	grotte
chairlift	téléseige
cliff	falaise
climbing	escalade
clip	mousquetonner
col	col
corner	diédre
crack	fissure
crag	école d'escalade
delicate	delicat
diagram	croquis
difficult	dur
difficulty	difficulté
dry	seche. sec

early	de bonne heure
east	est
easy	facile
edge	reglette
equipment	equipement
exposed (very)	aerienne (gazeux). expo
field(s)	pré paturage
first	premier
flake	ećaille
forbidden	interdit
friction	adherence
friend	friend
gear	materiel
gorge	gorges
grade	niveau. degré
grassy slope	pente en herbuese
groove	cannelure
gully	goulotte
heelhook	crochetage du pied
height	hauteur
helmet	casque
hold	prise
hole	trous
hut	refuge
interest	interêt
jam (a crack!)	coincement de
jug	gros prise
karabiner	mousqueton
knot	noeud
large	grand, gros

layback	position groupée
lead (a climb)	en tete
ledge	vire
limestone	calcaire
little	petit
long	long
lower (as in status)	inferieur
mantleshelf	technique de retablissement
map	carte
markings (to show the way)	balissage
niche	niche
north	nord
nuts	coinceurs
on-sight	a vue
overhang(ing)	surplomb(ante) dévers deversant
parking	parking
path	chemin
peg	piton
pocket	goute d'eau
point of aid	pointe d'aide
protection	assurage
quick-draw	degain
recommended (advice)	conseille
recommended (quality)	recommande
rescue	secours
rock	rocher
roof	toit
rope	corde
route	voie
rucksack	sac a dos
safety	securité

serious	engagé
shady	ombragé
single pitch climb	couenne
sit harness	baudrier-cuissard
slab	dalle
sling	sangle
south	sud
stance	relais
steep	raide
sunny	ensoleillé
take in	avale
technical	technique
tight rope	sec
top roping	en moulinette
topo	topo
track	chemin carrossable
traverse	traverse
upper	superior
varied	varie
vehicle	vehicle
very	tres
wall	mur (also dalle is used)
weekend	Le weekend
west	ouest

OTHER BOOKS ON THE FRENCH ALPS FROM CORDEE

THE HAUTE ROUTE CHAMONIX – ZERMATT

The Haute Route (Chamonix–Zermatt) was first walked in 1861 by members of the Alpine Club, and the first ski traverses were in 1903 and 1911. It is a unique expedition through the highest mountains of the Alps. Once the reserve of only the most determined Alpinists, modern equipment, huts and lifts have opened it up to any reAsonably fit and competent hillwalker, and in Spring to any steady parallel skier.

There are several variations – the Grande Lui and the Italian High Level Route being the hardest and especially recommended to strong parties.

The Guidebook covers the Classic Route, six main variations (both for walking and skiing), many additional minor route options, and the main mountains. It has:
● route descriptions and route diagrams. ● colour photographs, topo diagrams ● detailed descriptions for finding huts in bad weather ● 100 useful telephone numbers.
ISBN 1-871890-21-7

SUMMITS FOR ALL – 100 EASY MOUNTAINS FOR - WALKERS

Here is an extremely useful guide which will help you to follow the paths up 100 easy and beautiful mountains of Savoie and Haute-Savoie.
The information is wide ranging and will allow the walker to move easily from one mountain group to another, sampling the varied delights of the French Alps.
The routes on these mountains are not a serious challenge for experienced British hill walkers, they are indeed 'Summits for all'.
ISBN 1-871890-26-8

THE MONT BLANC RANGE TOPO GUIDE

83 clear topo-dirgrams with 203 descriptions of modern rock climbs on the Aiguilles de Chamonix, Aiguilles du Midi and Aiguilles Rouges.

MONT BLANC MASSIF Vol 1 (Alpine Club Guide Book)

Selected alpine routes and rock climbs from the Col de la Berangere to Col de Talefre.
ISBN 0-900523-57-3

MONT BLANC MASSIF Vol 2 (Alpine Club Guide Book)

Selected alpine routes and rock climbs from the Col de Talfre top the Swiss Val Ferret. Chamonix Aiguilles and Aiguilles Rouges.
ISBN 0-900523-58-1

WALKING THE GR5 –
LAKE GENEVA TO MONT BLANC

A guide with four colour IGN mapping to 650 kilometres of this famous Alpine footpath including the well known Tour du Mont Blanc and the Tour de la Vanoise GR5E (other titles in this series also available.)

THE PAYS DU MONT BLANC – Walking Tour

A new fully waymarked multi-day walking tour in the 'Haute Savoie' to rival the famous 'Tour du Mont Blanc'. Developed by the Federation Francaise de la Randonnee Pedestre and the regional tourist syndicate. Traverses the area of the Aiguilles Rouges and the high country to the south. Four colour IGN mapping in the established style of the GR guides.
ISBN 285 699 593 4

MONT BLANC TRAILS – Guide & Map

171 summer walks on well signposted and well maintained mountain footpaths in the Chamonix valley.
ISBN 2-910639-00-2

WALKING THE ALPINE PARKS OF FRANCE & - NORTHWEST ITALY

Complete details on over 100m trips through the uncrowded national and regional parks: Mercantour, Queyras, Ecrins Vanoise and Gran Paradiso.
ISBN 0-89886-398-8

FRENCH ROCK CLIMBS

Selected climbs in ten different locations chosen to give variety of styles of climbing in contrasting areas, visited in sequence the cliffs provide the basis of a logical tour, Saussois, le Gorge du Verdon, Buoux and more.
ISBN 0-904405-64-8

This is just a selection of many titles on outdoor recreation and travel stocked by Cordee. Please write for a copy of our comprehensive stocklist of books, maps and videos.
CORDEE, 3a De Montfort Street, Leicester, Great Britain LE1 7HD

Notes

Notes

Notes